Sowing into Tomorrow

Sowing into Tomorrow

A Guided Journal for Mothers

Stephanie Balke

Published by Sparrow Media, Hillsboro, OR
    (an imprint of Inscribe Press)
Cover design by Pelton Media Group,
    Fredericksburg, VA

Cover art and interior photography
    by Stephanie Balke

Printed in the United States of America

ISBN 978-1-951611-37-8 (print)
ISBN 978-1-951611-38-5 (eBook)

Contact the author at:
    stephanie.sparrow.media@gmail.com

Contents

Introduction I

The Journey 9

The Beginning 25

Process 41

Being Championed 49

Having Fun 69

Relationships 81

Pace 97

Being Influential 103

Who am I? III

Courage 125

Emotions 139

Accepting Help 153

Moving Forward 165

A Final Word 189

About the Author 193

Introduction

In the spring of 2013, a woman fought an intense battle for her health, her strength, and her future. Not only would this battle impact the woman's future, but also the future of her family.

So, what led to this day and why was it such a turning point?

In the years preceding her major turning point, a certain woman gradually increased the amount of responsibilities she held. These responsibilities were all good things, and many of them were focused on helping other people; but what had gone unnoticed was the woman's awareness of her need to pace herself and give herself grace.

The tipping point came when there was a change in her husband's work schedule. This change led the couple to working opposite shifts, which meant that the woman would hardly get to see her husband. She found herself knee deep in commitments to people outside of her family, and she didn't want to disappoint them. In hindsight, changes should have been made right away, but instead she kept barreling on. The woman found herself on a slippery slope of stress and anxiety. She didn't want to let anyone down, so she began to suffer. She was wilting inside, like a flower without water, but she continued to press on.

One night, she had lain down to sleep, but no sleep came. The same thing happened the next night, and the next; and eventually, a week had passed with barely any slumber. Her lack of sleep had become critical. Her anxiety was causing insomnia, and in return, the insomnia was causing anxiety.

She felt utterly stuck and helpless.

It was devastating.

The woman realized something would need to change if she was ever to have children. She sought out help, rested, took care of herself, and laid down all of her commitments outside of her family. She became well by changing the way that she lived. Both sleep and strength were returned to her; and the sun had started to shine in her heart again.

One year later, she was sharing the happy news with her husband that she was pregnant with their firstborn son.

So what happened in between this season of stress and the joy of having a child? How did she learn to live differently? The answer is found in these pages. It is the basis of this guided journal, and reflects on the woman's journey of weaving those truths into Motherhood. She gave value to her inner world, chose to persevere, gave herself time and space to process her thoughts and emotions, decided what it meant to be an influencer, found ways to have fun, put a high priority on key relationships, paced herself, chose courage in the face of difficult emotions, accepted help, and chose to forgive and move forward.

Who is this woman? This woman is me.

Why was this journal written?

Being a mother is an ongoing path of discovery and development. My hope for you as you journey through this journal is that you would find a sense of being able to take ownership of how you want to live and love.

In a sea of opinions, this journal is designed not to tell you what to do, but to help you delve deep and find your own voice. By finding your own voice, you can best lead the children in your life. And last, but by no means least, this journal is about you. You deserve to be nourished and valued just as much as the ones that you are nurturing.

How do I use this journal?

This journal is divided into 52 questions, one for every week of the year. However, you can feel free to go at a pace that works for you. Let your heart guide you in how to interact with this journal.

The questions are intentionally thought provoking; so allow yourself to be honest as you process through your answers.

You can keep your replies private, or share them with a trusted person, or process through them with a group of loving people. Because there are layers to every truth and lesson we learn in life, you may find yourself coming back to specific parts, or this entire journal repeatedly over the years.

Today, may you know hope that goes beyond reason.

May you experience deep wells of peace.

May you rest soundly.

May you dream sweet dreams.

May creativity flow from you,

And innovations fill your mind.

May kindness soak through into every part of your being.

May your relationships and friendships be strong and true,

And may you have the grace to live in today, with no worry for tomorrow.

The Journey

We are complex beings full of beauty, thought, creativity, and strength. A woman's strength is not to be undermined; it is deep and it is persistent. It is about her heart attitude, the focus of her will, her choice to never give up, her strength in the face of adversity and persecution, and her willingness to believe that she is inherently beautiful. A woman's courage and strength is based upon her inner world. Let us talk about our inner world, and how to cultivate it and treat it tenderly like a gardener tending her soil.

1. What makes you come alive? What makes your heart sing?

2. Look at your answers from question one and decide: what from this list would you like to weave into your life?

3. What frustrates or angers you?

4. Your answers for question three are clues to problems that you need to overcome, or issues that you are skilled at bringing justice into. What can you do about the things that anger and frustrate you?

_____

_____

_____

_____

_____

_____

_____

_____

_____

_____

5. Write down any obstacles you can see for moving forward in dealing with these frustrations.

_____

_____

_____

_____

_____

_____

_____

_____

_____

_____

The Beginning

Our journey requires perseverance in the choice to choose faithfulness.

Why? We will see the rewards for our actions in due time if we choose to not give up. Like a tree in winter, we may not see growth on the branches, but we know in the season to come, the leaves will grow. We would not cut down that tree in winter simply because its branches are bare. Our lives are about seasons and recognizing which season we are in.

6. Regarding being a mother, what season do you feel that you are most with your child/children?

7. What is rewarding about this season?

8. What is challenging about this season?

9. What are you hoping for in the seasons to come?

10. What can you do in this season that will cause your hopes for the future to come true?

Process

We need time to contemplate, to think, and to process. For some of us, we need an external outlet like a journal or a sketch pad. For others, it may be the listening ear of a trusted friend. Some people may be more comfortable mulling over their thoughts in their head. We need to give our hearts space to breathe, and time for our minds to unwind. Doing this process on a regular basis gives us a great perspective on our needs and hopes, and how we need to move forward in our decision making.

11. What way do you prefer to process your thoughts and feelings?

_____

_____

_____

_____

_____

_____

_____

_____

_____

_____

_____

_____

12. Are there any adjustments that you can make in the way that you process your thoughts and feelings?

Being Championed

Think for a moment about our human body. Where are the most vital organs located? They are hidden away beneath skin, bone, and tissue. Although these organs cannot be seen, we are unable to live without them. This can also be said about mothers. What we do is often not seen, but it is deeply essential. Our trials and our victories are often happening behind closed doors. Stay-at-home parents may feel particularly isolated from receiving affirmation. Not receiving applause in recognition does not make what we do any less important. You simply have to know that what you are doing is vital and choose to ignore anything that says otherwise. We choose what we listen to, what we read, and what we look at. The effects of what we take in can be subtle, but some influences that appear to be helpful actually leave us feeling like we are not good enough. This simply is not true. Parenting is a superhero role. So, find people who will champion you and help you on in this journey of Motherhood.

13. Do you feel like a superhero?

14. Make a list of all the things you do in support for others and then congratulate yourself.

15. Who do you have in your life that champions you?

16. Are there any influences in your life that cause you to feel less like a superhero and more like a failure?

17. What can you do to distance yourself from
these influences?

18. We need to recognize that changing what we choose to let influence us can be a step-by-step process. Give yourself the necessary time to make these changes, and record your thoughts and feelings about it here.

Having Fun

We need fun. Fun is especially crucial in the midst of or after a season of trial and pain. We need to feel childlike again. However, being childlike does not necessarily come easily to us as we carry many responsibilities. Despite everything that has the capacity to weigh us down, we need to capture the moments where we can simply have fun. How is this possible while having young children and babies in our homes? How are we able to do this when we are needed by them day and night, and live in a sleep deprived state? These questions can be asked by any woman who has a demanding role in life. The way to move forward is by finding fun things to do that are simple and easy so that we can weave them into our daily lives.

19. What do you find fun?

20. Are you currently having any fun?

21. If more fun is needed, what simple steps can you take to weave fun into your life?

22. Who can support you in your need for fun? Talk to them.

_____

_____

_____

_____

_____

_____

_____

_____

_____

_____

_____

_____

Relationships

There is a mystery to relationships, whether it is family, friendship, or romantic; love is not easily defined or measured. It is like the wind, you can feel it, but you cannot see it. It is wild and mysterious. Relationships cannot be put in boxes or easily measured by a set of linear rules. Relationships are more like a winding path with gates, valleys, and mountaintops.

When our life-giving relationships are nurtured, then wonder, beauty, and joy are produced. So how do we nurture relationships? Think of our relationships like plants; they thrive from the consistent care of regular watering. They do not necessarily need a huge amount of water at once, but consistency is the key. This principle can also be applied to relationships. We need to be consistent with each other. Regular attention given to someone we care about causes the relationship to thrive and grow, and over time, become deeply rooted and strong, just like a mature plant.

What else can we do to nurture the key relationships in our life? Give them time and space to grow. Have you ever noticed how the most delightful moments in a relationship often happen in a relaxed and unstructured settings? These are times when we are not hurrying from one task to the next, and when we do not have to constantly watch the clock. Certainly, having a schedule and being on time are important, but the key here is to allow yourself and your loved ones time to breathe and unwind. It is here in this place that our hearts can be knitted together.

23. Who do you share life-giving relationships
with in your life?

24. Are there relationships in your life that are not life giving?

25. What adjustments do you need to make so that you are receiving from life-giving relationships?

26. There is a difference between a relationship that is toxic and a relationship where the other person needs you to pour life into their heart. Identify any of these relationships here.

27. How can you make time for the relationships in your life where you are being poured into or you are pouring into others?

Pace

Life can be full of surprises. We can make good choices and still find ourselves in the midst of challenging circumstances. We live in villages, towns, cities, and nations, where the actions of others or even the weather can cause us to face testing times. What shall we do about this? It is important for us to pace ourselves, to regularly find time to get our inner reservoir poured into, so that we have inner reserves when they are needed.

It can be so tempting to live our lives at full throttle because it can look more impressive to those around us. When we are doing or producing a lot, it draws attention and praise. Praise is not wrong, but if praise is what drives us, then we may want to consider our pace of life. Are we running so hard that when adversity comes we have nothing left to enable us to stand strong in the storm?

28. Are you living your life at full throttle?

29. Are there any changes that you need to make to give yourself a more manageable pace of life?

_____

_____

_____

_____

_____

_____

_____

_____

_____

_____

Being Influential

What does it mean to be influential?
Influence begins with those closest to
us: our family, closest friends, and our co-
workers. The people that we spend the most
time with are the most influential. It can be so
easy to believe that influence is measured by
numbers, but it is more accurately measured
by real and lasting change. We often have a
choice between influencing a small group
of people in a deep and profound way, or
influencing a large group of people in a small
and shallower way. Of course, it is possible
to both love our family and friends and
influence large groups of people; but when
faced with a choice, what will we choose?

30. In what areas of your life do you feel
most influential?

31. Do you need to make any changes to prioritize those closest to you?

Who Am I?

Comparison is so easy to slip into. It often seems normal to think out of comparison, but it is dangerous because it is deeply unfair. Two people may look or sound similar on the outside, but have come from hugely different life circumstances. Many people have had to push through, and overcome huge obstacles to do things that others consider normal. It is not the fault of the person who has had less to deal with; they are not the villain in this story. It simply comes down to the fact that we are all born into and experience different life circumstances.

What defines you is what you do with your life circumstances. It is possible to overcome the turmoil and difficulties that seem insurmountable, and when you do, you have the advantage of seeing life from a perspective that is rich with victory and wisdom.

32. Do you feel that you compare yourself to others?

33. What have you overcome in your life?

34. How can you focus on your victories?

35. How can you be kind to yourself?

Courage

What do we do when it is painful to face
what is in our heart? What do we do when
our heart aches with hurt, screams with anger,
or trembles with fear? It can be so easy to
try and avoid these feelings as they are very
uncomfortable. It takes courage to process
through these emotions. Besides facing our
emotions, our other options are to harden
our hearts and become a cold and unfeeling
human; or stuff these unwanted emotions,
which leads to larger problems down the road.
Our hearts are alive and vibrant, and ignoring
them does not make them go away. Ignoring
what our heart needs is described as "bottling
it up." Our heart is like a carbonated drink,
when it is repeatedly shaken and then opened
up, it will explode. We may explode in anger
and pain, which leads to hurting ourselves or
our relationships. Over time, we may even

become physically ill or have an emotional and mental breakdown.

Therefore, imagine that your heart is like a garden. Tend to it regularly with tender loving care. You deserve to be loved, including by yourself. We need a healthy dose of self-care, especially when we are mothering others. The role of a mother can be a demanding one, so do not ignore your heart's needs. Take a deep breath, hold onto courage, and do what you need to do to move through pain, anger, and fear, into a brighter tomorrow.

36. Take courage and think about this question: do you want to live with a heart that is free, or one that is tied up?

37. What emotions do you need to face and process through?

38. Who can walk this journey towards a free heart with you?

39. What steps do you need to take to move forward?

Emotions

Why do we need to be encouraged that it is alright to be sad? There can be a lot of pressure to give off the illusion that we feel fine all the time, but this is not real. Sadness is an indicator. It may be showing that you care very deeply for someone, and the tenderness of your heart is causing you to feel sad at their distress. Sadness may indicate that something deeply painful has happened to you, and you are processing that grief. It may be that you care about more than just yourself, and so when you see disheartening news, you are affected.

Sadness is different than depression. Depression is like a heavy and suffocating blanket that you cannot shift off from your shoulders. You need help when you suffer from depression, and there is no shame in seeking that help.

Sadness is a normal human emotion, and by denying it, you are not expressing the whole of your heart. You do not have to stay in sadness, but it is important to process through it and recognize why it is there so that you can come out the other side experiencing joy.

40. Is there anything that you feel sad about?

41. What can you do to process any feelings of sadness?

42. Is there anything you need to do to address issues or circumstances that are causing you to feel sad?

_____

_____

_____

_____

_____

_____

_____

_____

_____

_____

_____

43. Are there any areas of sadness where you need to let it go because it is weighing on your heart in an unnecessary way?

Accepting Help

What do we do when adversity comes our way or when we feel overwhelmed? Being a mother can be conducive to feeling overwhelmed, especially when our children are young. Children have so many needs that they are not able to meet by themselves that we are responsible for. Therefore, what we do is incredibly important; but what do we do when the responsibilities weigh on us? What do we do when we need to admit that it is hard sometimes, or we need to ask for help? Have we failed? Should we be embarrassed?

No. We have not failed, and we have no reason to feel shame. It is normal to need help. We are not meant to live alone and isolated like an island. So what do we do when we feel a strong urge to isolate ourselves? Why do we isolate ourselves? Why do we feel the need to keep up the appearance that we are fine all of the time? It is because we fear rejection. Although there is rejection in this world, there is acceptance too. To be accepted in our time of need forms the deep bonds of friendship and love. Adversity tends to have a way of pushing people together. It is the silver lining on a dark cloud. So, take courage. Let your needs be known. If someone rejects you in your time of need, know that others will accept you and that you will gain the help that you need.

44. Where do you need help?

45. Are you willing to make the choice to be real?

_____

_____

_____

_____

_____

_____

_____

_____

_____

_____

_____

_____

46. Who in your life can you trust to share your need for help and support in a real way?

_____

_____

_____

_____

_____

_____

_____

_____

_____

_____

_____

_____

Moving Forward

When we are rejected by someone in our time of need, it hurts. It is deeply unjust. What do we do with the feelings that arise either from the present or the past? In one word, it is forgiveness. Just mentioning the word forgiveness can send a shudder down our spine. We can feel angry at just the mention of it! Why should I forgive? Well, let's take a look at what forgiveness is.

Is it saying that the other person was right? No.

Is it saying that it doesn't matter what they did to us? No.

Is it saying that they do not deserve any consequences for their actions? No.

Forgiveness is a choice of our will to not

hold the pain and the anger inside of our heart anymore. It is a choice to free ourselves from the lasting effects of what others have done to us. It is a choice towards inner healing and freedom. Is it easy? No. Will we always feel like forgiving? Probably not.

Is it worth it? Absolutely yes! Forgiveness is truly the only way forward. To not forgive keeps us living in the pain of our past. If you want a brighter future, you are going to need to forgive. It takes time, and often needs to be done repeatedly. Whenever we feel the sting of pain, or the anger well up within us, we need to choose to forgive and keep forgiving until the sting goes away. Then all we are left with are memories that do not have the power to trigger us anymore; and we can live a much happier life. You are choosing to be victorious when you choose to forgive.

47. Are you willing to forgive?

48. Who do you need to forgive?

49. Do you need the support of a trusted person to help you move forward on a path of forgiveness?

50. Do you need to forgive yourself for anything?

51. Remember to have fun even in the midst of processing tough emotions. What are you doing that is fun?

52. What can you permanently weave into your life that will keep you moving forward on a path towards a free and happy heart? Who can you share your journey with that would benefit from what you have discovered?

Additional Notes

A Final Word

For the love of chocolate
(An invitation to taste of goodness)

Growing up in England, I was familiar with European chocolate, with my favorite being from Switzerland. It is a rich, deep, melt in your mouth kind of experience. And then I came to America, and one day as a token of friendship I was offered some chocolate which is hugely popular in the USA. Its name shall remain anonymous, but to me it tasted bland, dull and a little like eating cardboard. It simply did not compare to the delights of Swiss chocolate! It was awful, and to this day I refuse to eat it.

We all have associations towards things, or people, based on our experiences. This treasure trove of moments and memories serves us to make wise decisions in the future. For example, I am now equipped to make wise choices when choosing chocolate.

During my childhood I had mixed experiences not only of various European chocolates, but also of religion and faith. I encountered those who professed the name of Jesus, but showed little love, and actually demonstrated a controlling and harsh religion. And then I also knew those who were beacons of light and love, demonstrating their faith in a true and genuine way. They too spoke of following Jesus. How could these two groups both truly know Jesus?

This passage from the Bible helps me understand the difference, and the true meaning of love.

> 1 John 4:7-9 (New Living Translation) "Dear friends, let us continue to love one another, for love comes from God. Anyone who loves is a child of God and knows God. But anyone who does not love does not know God, for God is love. God showed how much he loved us by sending his one and only Son into the world so that we might have eternal life through him."

It has been my growing experience over the years that these words in the Bible are true, and what they speak of is a source of life to me.

It may be that you have only ever tasted the awful kind of chocolate, or the harsh and hypocritical kind of religion practiced in the name of Jesus. This would understandably turn you away from chocolate or Jesus. But what if there is a different experience to be had? What if these words from the Bible are true? What if there really is a source of endless and unconditional love? Surely we need that in our daily lives, in our hearts, and homes, as we Mother our children.

I would love to hear from you. Please write to me at: stephanie.sparrow.media@gmail.com

About the Author

Stephanie is a writer, photographer, artist, and Gemological Institute of America accredited jewelry professional, but most of all a Mom. She grew up in England, and now lives in California  with her husband and two sons. She loves the beauty of nature and gemstones, and sipping from a cup of hot tea. Her website is www. stephaniebalke.com.